KU-428-706

ANCIENT GREECE

Written by Anita Ganeri

W

FRANKLIN WATTS

LONDON•SYDNEY

Franklin Watts
First published in Great Britain in 2017
by The Watts Publishing Group
Copyright © The Watts Publishing Group, 2017
All rights reserved.

Editor: Sarah Silver
Designer: Matt Lilly
Picture researcher: Diana Morris

ISBN 978 1 4451 5306 3

abxyz/Dreamstime: 12c. Anastasios71/Shutterstock: front cover, 18c, 18bl. Erin Babnik/Alamy: 24b. © The Trustees of the British Museum. All Rights Reserved: 21t. H M Brock/Mullan Collection/Mary Evans PL: 15. Anton Chygarev/Dreamstime: 6t. Classic Image/Alamy: 27b. De Agostini/Superstock: 9b. Gimas/Shutterstock: 14t. Greek Photonews/Alamy: 24c. Panagiotis Karapanagiotis/Dreamstime: 10b. Kmiragaya/Dreamstime: 28b. Robyn MacKenzie/Dreamstime: 23cl. Megastocker/Dreamstime: 3, 20t. Mineria6/Dreamstime: 19t. Mr 1805/Dreamstime: 28c. Edwin Mullan/Chronicle/Alamy: 26. Mytime/Dreamstime: 12b. Nick Pavlakis/Shutterstock: 22b. Pecold/Shutterstock: 13b. Angela N Perryman/Shutterstock: 14b. Pjr Travel/Alamy: 17b. prapass/Shutterstock: 11b, 17t, 23cr, 29t. Michael Rosskothen/Shutterstock: 25. Lisa S/Shutterstock: 10t. Sborisov/Dreamstime: 6b. Antonio Scorza/Shutterstock: 27t. Smoxx/Shutterstock: 21b. Tas Photo/Dreamstime: 5. Favrizio Troiani/Dreamstime: 7b. Tupungato/Shutterstock: 19cr. University of Pennsylvania/Wikimedia Commons: 9c. urbanzon/Shutterstock: 18br. Repina Valeriya/Shutterstock: 20b. Vasilis Ververidis/Shutterstock: 23b. Vasily Voropaev/Shutterstock: 16t, 16b, 22t, 22c, 29c. Claudio Zaccherini/Shutterstock: 19c. Oleg Znamenskiy/Shutterstock: 7t. Zwiebackesser/Shutterstock: 13t.

Every attempt has been made to clear copyright. Should there be any inadvertent omission please apply to the publisher for rectification.

FSC
www.fsc.org
MIX
Paper from
responsible sources
FSC® C104740

Printed in China

Franklin Watts
An imprint of
Hachette Children's Group
Part of The Watts Publishing Group
Carmelite House
50 Victoria Embankment
London EC4Y 0DZ

An Hachette UK Company
www.hachette.co.uk

www.franklinwatts.co.uk

DUDLEY SCHOOLS LIBRARY SERVICE	
S00000799271	
£12.99	J938
02-Nov-2017	PETERS

Contents

Who were the ancient Greeks?

The ancient Greeks were the people who lived in Greece around 2,500 years ago. They were great thinkers, scientists, writers and politicians. They developed a new way of life and left behind many ideas that other people have admired and copied. The ancient Greek era ended in around 146 BCE, when Greece was conquered by the Romans.

The Greek world

Greece is made up of a mainland, and hundreds of islands in the Ionian and Aegean seas. It is a mountainous country, and this led many ancient Greeks to leave their homeland and set up colonies around the coasts of the Mediterranean Sea. Sailing to find new lands, and also on trading expeditions, the Greeks spread their culture to many other places.

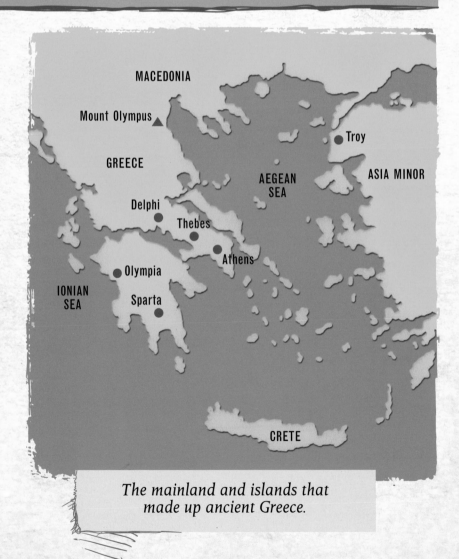

The mainland and islands that made up ancient Greece.

Ancient Greece

Around 2000–1450 BCE	The Minoan civilisation flourishes on Crete
Around 1600–1100 BCE	The Mycenaeans dominate mainland Greece
1200s BCE	The Trojan War between Greece and Troy
1100 BCE	Greece enters a 'dark age'
800s BCE	Many Greeks sail off to set up colonies
776 BCE	The first Olympic Games are held at Olympia
490–449 BCE	The Persian Wars between Greece and Persia
Around 480 BCE	The age of Classical Greece begins
431–404 BCE	The Peloponnesian War between Athens and Sparta
Around 146 BCE	The Romans conquer Greece

GREEK HISTORY

Herodotus (c. 484–425 BCE) was a Greek historian who wrote a long account of the Persian Wars (see pages 26–27), based on interviews with survivors. It is still one of our main sources for understanding life in the Greek world at that time. Herodotus was also a great traveller. He wrote about his many journeys, to Egypt and beyond, including descriptions of unusual things he had seen or heard of, such as mummies and crocodiles.

WRITING HISTORY

Much of what we know about history comes from written accounts and records that have been left behind. Throughout this book, you will find panels asking you to write your own versions of the history you have read. You will find the information you need in the book, but you can also look online and in other books. Use the tips provided, and don't be afraid to let your imagination run wild.

A statue of the great Greek historian, Herodotus.

Ancient Greek life

The first great civilisation in Greece flourished on the island of Crete around 2000–1450 BCE. Named after their legendary king, Minos, the Minoans grew rich from trade. They built splendid towns and palaces, which were later destroyed by earthquakes. By about 1450 BCE, people from mainland Greece had taken control of Crete. They were called the Mycenaeans. The Mycenaeans were great traders and warriors – many examples of weapons and armour have been found in Mycenaean graves.

Classical Greece

From around 480 BCE, Greece entered a 'golden age' when its culture was at its height. Historians call this period Classical Greece. During this time, the Greeks built many grand monuments, and art, literature and learning thrived. The Greeks also established a new form of government, called democracy (see page 9), and fought many great wars.

The ruins of the Palace of Knossos on the island of Crete.

The Parthenon, in Athens, was built during Greece's golden age.

Greeks at home

Wealthy ancient Greeks lived in houses, constructed of sun-dried mud bricks, built around a central courtyard. They had small windows, with wooden shutters that could be closed to keep the house cool. Inside, men and women had separate rooms, and there were also living quarters for the family's slaves.

Olive trees grew well in the poor soil. People ate the olives or crushed them to make olive oil.

Farms and food

Most ancient Greeks were farmers, even though the mountainous landscape and dry climate made growing crops difficult. A typical farm was small and only produced enough food for a single family. Meals were fairly simple. For breakfast, there was barley bread dipped in wine. Lunch might be bread, cheese and olives or figs. For dinner, most people ate barley porridge, with eggs, fish and vegetables. Only rich people could afford to eat meat.

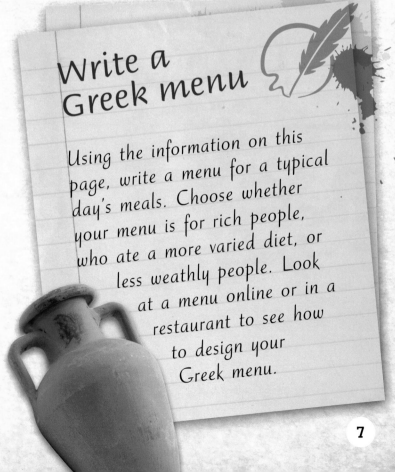

Write a Greek menu

Using the information on this page, write a menu for a typical day's meals. Choose whether your menu is for rich people, who ate a more varied diet, or less weathly people. Look at a menu online or in a restaurant to see how to design your Greek menu.

Αα	Ββ	Γγ	Δδ	Εε	Ζζ	Ηη	Θθ
alpha	beta	gamma	delta	epsilon	zeta	eta	theta

Ιι	Κκ	Λλ	Μμ	Νν	Ξξ	Οο	Ππ
iota	kappa	lamda	mu	nu	xi	omicron	pi

Ρρ	Σσ	Ττ	Υυ	Φφ	Χχ	Ψψ	Ωω
rho	sigma	tau	upsilon	phi	chi	psi	omega

The Greek alphabet has 24 letters, from alpha to omega. Greek letters, such as pi, are still used as mathematical symbols today.

Language and writing

The ancient Greeks spoke the same language, although each region had its own dialect. Their alphabet was based on that of the Phoenicians, with whom the Greeks traded. The Phoenician alphabet only used consonants – the Greeks added vowels.

Did you know?

Many of the words we use in English come from ancient Greek, especially in science and technology. Some words are made up of two Greek words joined together.

geography = description of the Earth
alphabet = alpha + beta (the first two letters of the Greek alphabet)
photography = light + drawing
telescope = far + to look
hippopotamus = river + horse x 6
astronomy = stars + law (law of the stars)

LOST MANUSCRIPTS

Ancient Greek writers produced a huge number of works. In the late 19th century, archaeologists discovered thousands of long-lost Greek manuscripts in an ancient rubbish dump in Egypt. They included letters, plays and poems.

A fragment of an ancient Greek manuscript found in Egypt.

Greek society

Greek society was split into two main groups of people – free men and slaves. In Athens, free men were either citizens (men born in Athens) or metics (men born elsewhere). Only citizens could have a say in the government (see below), own land or speak in a law court. These social divisions only applied to men. Greek women did not have any rights.

People power

Until the early 500s BCE, most Greek states were ruled by small groups of wealthy landowners, called aristocrats. Ordinary people resented their power, and a new system of government was introduced in Athens. It was called 'democracy' which means 'rule by the people'. For the first time, it gave every citizen a say in how their city was governed.

Did you know?

In Athens, people could remove unpopular politicians by using a process called ostracism. The person's name was scratched on a piece of broken pottery, called an *ostrakon*. If more than 6,000 people named the same politician, he was banished from the city for ten years.

City states

Ancient Greece was made up of many small 'city-states', with their own governments, armies and laws. The two most powerful were deadly rivals: Athens and Sparta.

Athens was named after Athena, the goddess of war and wisdom.

🏛 Athens 🏛

Athens was the biggest city-state. A leading centre for learning, arts and trade, it had its own port at Piraeus, and the largest navy in Greece. The city was famous for its grand buildings, including the Parthenon (see page 6). This beautiful temple stood on a rocky hill, called the Acropolis.

🏛 Sparta 🏛

The city of Sparta was famous for its tough soldiers. From the age of seven, Spartan boys were sent to army training camps where they learned boxing, wrestling and spear-throwing. To harden them up, they were forced to sleep outside, in all weathers, and to steal food. If they were caught, they were flogged – to teach them the importance of cunning.

Every Spartan boy was expected to become a warrior.

Design a poster

You're in charge of finding recruits for a new army camp in Sparta. Design a poster advertising your camp. Remember to say what sort of boys you are looking for, and what they can expect to learn. Add a catchy headline to attract attention.

Writing History:

A postcard from Athens

Imagine that you are spending a few days in Athens. You've travelled from your village in the countryside to stay with your uncle. It is your first time in a big city, and you have been busy sightseeing. You decide to write a postcard to your parents, telling them about some of the things you have seen. The opening of the postcard has already been written.

WRITING HINTS AND TIPS

- Use chatty, informal language for writing your postcard.
- Pick out the most important points – you haven't got much space.
- Make sure that you leave room for the address.
- Write another postcard from Sparta. How different will it be?

Tuesday 9th May

Hi Mum and Dad!
Having a brilliant
time in Athens. It's
an amazing place!
Went sightseeing
today ...

To Philippos and Eulalia
Eleusis Village
Near Athens
Attica
Greece

Beliefs and myths

The ancient Greeks believed in many gods and goddesses who watched over the world, and sometimes interfered in what people were doing. In many ways, the gods were like humans. They fell in love, got married, quarrelled and fought. But they were also all-powerful and immortal, and needed to be honoured and respected.

The 12 Olympians

The 12 most important gods and goddesses were called the Olympians. They rose to power after a long war against the Titans. Zeus was king of the gods, and ruler of the heavens. His wife was Hera, goddess of women and marriage. Zeus's children included Apollo, the sun god; Artemis, goddess of the moon; and Athena, goddess of wisdom, war and Athens.

This bust of Zeus is on display in the Vatican Museum, Italy.

The Olympians were believed to live on Mount Olympus, the highest mountain in Greece.

The Underworld

The Greeks believed that the souls of the dead went to the Underworld. It was ruled by the god, Pluto (Zeus's brother). To reach the Underworld, a soul had to cross the River Styx. At funerals, a coin was placed in the dead person's mouth to pay Charon, the ferryman. If they did not have a coin, they were doomed to wander forever on the riverbank.

Charon, rowing his ferry across the river.

Did you know?

A monstrous three-headed dog, called Cerberus, guarded the gates to the Underworld. His job was to stop anyone leaving the land of the dead, and to prevent living intruders from entering. He was finally captured by Heracles, as one of his 12 labours (see page 16), and was dragged, in chains, up to Earth. He later escaped and returned to his deadly duties.

Pluto, god of the dead, with Cerberus, the three-headed guard of the Underworld.

Write an interview

Imagine that you are interviewing Charon, the ferryman. What sort of questions would you ask him about his job? Write up your interview as a series of questions and answers. Make the questions and answers short and snappy.

This temple, dedicated to the goddess Athena, is at the ancient Greek colony Paestum, in Italy.

Worship and temples

The Greeks built splendid temples as the gods' homes on Earth. If people were ill or in trouble, they went to the temple to ask the gods for help. They took money, jewellery, food and wine as gifts to please the gods. The Greeks also worshipped at home at their family altar.

Did you know?

The Greeks put statues of the gods inside their temples. A magnificent statue of the goddess, Athena, stood in the Parthenon in Athens. Made from gold and ivory, it was over 12 m tall. The gold was later used to pay the army, and replaced by cheaper bronze.

You can still see the remains of Apollo's Temple at Delphi today.

Oracle at Delphi

Before the Greeks began anything important, such as a journey, they tried to find out the will of the gods. Often, they visited an oracle, where a priest or priestess spoke on a god's behalf. The most famous oracle was at Delphi where the god, Apollo, spoke through his priestess. People came from all over Greece to put their questions to the priestess.

Myths and heroes

The Greeks had many stories about their gods and heroes. One myth tells how Theseus travelled to Crete to kill a terrible, bull-headed monster, called the Minotaur. The Minotaur lived in the Labyrinth, a maze so confusing that no one ever found their way out again. The king's daughter, Ariadne, gave Theseus a ball of thread. As he entered the Labyrinth, he tied one end to the entrance, and was able to follow it out again.

Jason and the golden fleece

Another myth tells of Jason, who set out in his great ship, the Argo, to find the priceless golden fleece. His journey was filled with danger, including navigating through gigantic cliffs that crushed ships by slamming shut. Finally, helped by the king's daughter, Medea, Jason seized the fleece from the dragon that guarded it and sailed for home.

EPIC POEM

The Argonautica is a long Greek poem, written by Apollonius Rhodius in the third century BCE. It tells the myth of Jason but with a twist. Apollonius's readers already knew the story so he concentrated instead on the love affair between Jason and Medea.

Helped by Medea, Jason was able to take the golden fleece home and claim his throne.

Heracles, superhero

The most famous Greek hero was Heracles (known to the Romans as Hercules) who performed 12 seemingly impossible tasks, as punishment for killing his family.

The Twelve Tasks of Heracles

1. Kill a man-eating lion with skin so tough that no weapon could pierce it.
2. Kill the hydra, a monster with nine heads and poisonous breath.
3. Catch a deer with golden horns that ran so fast it could outrun an arrow.
4. Trap a ferocious boar. Heracles drove the boar into a thick drift of snow.
5. Clean King Augeus' stables in one day. They had not been cleaned for 30 years.
6. Defeat a flock of man-eating birds with sharp bronze beaks and feathers.
7. Catch the gigantic bull of Crete that ran wild, causing great damage.
8. Round up a herd of wild horses that fed on human flesh.
9. Fetch a belt belonging to Hippolyta, a warrior-queen.
10. Fetch a herd of cattle, belonging to a fearsome giant.
11. Steal the golden apples that belonged to the goddess, Hera.
12. Bring Cerberus (see page 13) back from the Underworld.

Write a cartoon strip

Choose one of the myths you've read on the last few pages, and turn it into a cartoon strip. Pick out the main events in the story first, so that you know how many picture frames you will need. Add speech bubbles and text flashes to help the story along.

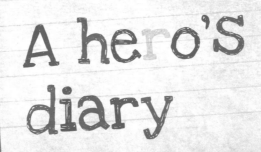

A hero's diary

Imagine that you are Heracles, writing a diary about the tasks you have to perform. The first entry has already been written. Can you write the rest? Don't forget to describe each task and also to say how Heracles felt about it. Which did he find the most difficult or dangerous? Did he worry about not being able to complete them all?

Friday

Well, today's task was to kill a lion. Easier said than done. This was no ordinary animal. It had a terrible reputation for eating people, and I could easily have ended up as lunch. Trouble is my arrows just bounced off its fur, so it was lucky that I'd brought my club along!

WRITING HINTS AND TIPS

- Write your diary in chronological order (the order in which things happen).
- You don't have to write down everything that happens — pick out the most interesting things.
- Write your diary in the first person — put yourself in Heracles' place.
- Include your thoughts and feelings about the things that have happened.
- Your diary is for your eyes only, so you can write whatever you like!

As one of his tasks, Heracles had to catch a giant bull.

Learning and leisure

The ancient Greeks were great thinkers and scholars. At first, they believed that everything in nature was the work of the gods. Later, they tried to find more logical and scientific ways of making sense of the world. Greek scholars were called philosophers, which means 'lovers of knowledge'. Their ideas and theories are still studied and used today.

Greek scholars

Plato (c. 428–348 BCE)

Plato was Socrates' greatest student, and was famous for his work on government and politics. Among other things, he wrote about the ideal way of governing a city-state.

Socrates (c. 469–399 BCE)

Socrates taught by asking his students questions to encourage them to think more deeply. But his ideas made him unpopular, and he was forced to take his own life by drinking poison.

Aristotle (c. 384–322 BCE)

Aristotle wrote mainly about politics and society, but also about science, music, languages and poetry. His ideas about natural history were followed for more than a thousand years.

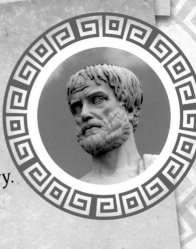

Hippocrates
(c. 460–370 BCE)

Hippocrates took a scientific approach to medicine, examining patients carefully and making a diagnosis. Doctors still follow his code of ethics, called the Hippocratic Oath.

Pythagoras
(c. 570–495 BCE)

Pythagoras is still famous for the mathematical theorem (rule) that takes his name. It allows you to calculate the length of the third side of any right-angled triangle.

Archimedes
(c. 287–212 BCE)

Archimedes discovered an important law of physics — that an object displaces its own volume of water. He is said to have noticed this when he was sitting in the bath.

Write an obituary

An obituary is a news article that reports the recent death of an important person. Try writing an obituary for one of the Greek scholars on these two pages. Include their dates of birth and death, and some information about their life and achievements. Try to give the reader an idea of what the person might have been like.

Theatre trip

In ancient Greece, going to the theatre was very popular. Songs and dances featured as part of religious festivals. At first, they were performed in the market place. Later, large, open-air theatres were built. Most Greek cities had a theatre that could seat thousands of people. The audience sat in a semi-circle around the stage so that everyone had a good view.

The great theatre at Epidaurus could seat 14,000 people.

Actors and masks

All ancient Greek actors were men or boys — women were not allowed to act. The actors wore painted masks made from stiffened cloth, with wigs of human or animal hair. Facial features were exaggerated so that they were easy to see. To change character, an actor simply changed his mask.

Masks were worn to show which character each actor was playing.

Plays and playwrights

Greeks plays were either comedies or tragedies. They were so popular that playwrights, such as Sophocles, Euripides and Aristophanes, were treated as celebrities. An annual drama competition was held in Athens, with prizes for the best actors and playwrights. Sophocles was one of the most successful writers of tragedy. He took part in around 30 competitions and came first 18 times.

Stone tokens were used as theatre tickets.

PLAY FOR TODAY

In his lifetime, Sophocles wrote around 120 tragedies. Only seven have survived, but these are still performed in theatres around the world today. The most famous are called the Theban plays. These three plays tell of the fate of the city of Thebes during the reign of the mythical king, Oedipus.

Write a Greek play review

Using the information in this chapter, try writing a review of a Greek play. Start by saying what you saw, then give a short summary of the play. Talk about the performance — how good were the actors? Finish off with your overall impression — would you recommend the play to others? You could also include a star rating or a thumbs up/thumbs down.

Sophocles was one of the greatest playwrights of ancient Greece.

Sporting heroes

Sport was very important in ancient Greece as a way of keeping fit for war. There were many sporting competitions. The most important were the Olympic Games which began in 776 BCE. Held every four years in Olympia, in honour of Zeus, the Games attracted athletes from all over Greece.

DAY-TO-DAY AT THE GAMES

Day 1:

Athletes and trainers swear the Olympic oath.

Boys' running, wrestling and boxing contests.

Day 2:

Horse and chariot races.

Pentathlon
(running, wrestling, long jump, discus and javelin).

Day 3:

Sacrifice of oxen to Zeus.

Running races:
dolichos (20–24 lengths of the track), *diaulos* (two lengths), *stade* (one length).

Day 4:

Contact sports – wrestling, boxing and pankration (boxing and wrestling combined).

Day 5:

Presentation of olive-leaf crowns to winning athletes.

Farewell feast.

Did you know?

Any athlete caught cheating at the Games – perhaps by bribing his competitors to let him win – had to pay a large fine. This was used to pay for bronze statues of Zeus which were placed by the entrance to the stadium. As a warning, they were labelled with the cheats' names.

Wrestling was a very popular event at the Olympic Games.

Writing History:

An athlete's blog

Imagine that you are an athlete, taking part in the Olympic Games. You're competing in pankration, the final and deadliest event. Write a blog about your time in Olympia. The first post has already been written. Using the information on page 22, can you write the rest?

Articles | Control Panel | View My Blog | Documentation | Log Out

15 July 316 BCE 18.30

OLYMPIA, HERE I COME!

Written by **Exinetos**

What a day! After a long march and months of training, I've made it to my first Olympics. Finally! It's a dream come true. First up was swearing the Olympic oath. Then I watched the boys' wrestling — some of those youngsters are really good. Now I've got a few days to wait until my event, so I'm going to do some exploring and check out the competition.

The site of the first Olympic Games in Olympia, Greece.

WRITING HINTS AND TIPS

- Write a new post every day — each post can be quite short.
- Grab your reader's attention with your first few sentences.
- Don't forget to start each post with the date and time.
- Use informal language that is friendly and chatty.
- Remember to include your own feelings about what has happened.

Greeks at war

In ancient Greece, each city-state had its own army that could be called on in times of war. In Athens, young men spent two years in military training, and could be called up from the age of 20. The Athenian army was led by ten commanders, called *strategoi*, who were elected by the citizens. One or two strategoi were sent out with each military expedition.

Hoplites in action

The most important part of a Greek army were the foot-soldiers, called hoplites. Hoplites wore bronze helmets, breastplates and leg guards, and were armed with long spears, swords and round shields. They fought in a formation, called a phalanx. Many rows of hoplites formed a block, with their shields held in front. In battle, the phalanx charged forward, smashing into the enemy.

A re-enactor dressed as a hoplite in full armour.

In a phalanx, flute music was played to help the men keep in step.

Greek warships

Greek warships were called triremes. They were long, narrow, easy to manoeuvre, and very fast. They had sails and oars, with three rows of oarsmen on either side. There were two long steering oars at the back.

At the front was a sharp, metal point, or ram. The main battle tactic was to steer straight at an enemy ship so that the ram smashed a hole in its side, and it filled with water, and sank.

For many years, triremes were the most successful warships in the Mediterranean.

Battle of Salamis

In 480 BCE, a great sea battle took place off the coast of Salamis between the Greeks and the Persians (see page 26). The Greek navy was heavily outnumbered but managed to trick the Persian ships into sailing into a narrow channel where they became trapped. The Greek ships attacked, claiming a famous victory.

Did you know?

A trireme needed 170 men to row it – one man to each oar. These oarsmen were free citizens, not slaves. In peacetime, they practised long and hard, becoming expert rowers. On board, it took great skill for them all to keep in time and power the ship forward. Historians think pipe music may have been played to help them.

The Persian Wars

The Greek city-states were often at war with each other but, occasionally, they put their quarrels aside to unite against a foreign enemy, especially the Persians (from modern-day Iran). In 490 BCE, the Persians invaded Greece, beginning 40 years of war.

> *The hoplites helped to win the Battle of Marathon for the Greeks.*

Write an acrostic poem

Write an acrostic poem about Greek battles, using the word 'MARATHON'. Write the letters in a line down the side of the page. Then use the first letter of each line to start a word or phrase. The words don't have to make a proper sentence. Some can be just adjectives or nouns.

Battle of Marathon

One of the greatest battles of the Persian Wars was the Battle of Marathon in 490 BCE. Despite being outnumbered by the Persians, the Greeks won the battle. A Greek messenger, Pheidippides, ran 42 km non-stop to Athens to deliver the good news. Incredibly, he had already run for two days, from Athens to Sparta, to fetch help.

Did you know?

Pheidippides' amazing feat was the inspiration for the modern marathon race. It is 42.195 km long, almost the same distance as Pheidippides ran. It was one of the original events held at the first modern Olympic Games in 1896.

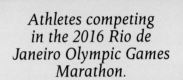

Athletes competing in the 2016 Rio de Janeiro Olympic Games Marathon.

The Peloponnesian War

From 431–404 BCE, Athens and Sparta faced each other in a long and deadly war. After years of fighting, the Spartans struck a decisive blow. At the Battle of Aegospotami in 405 BCE, they defeated the mighty Athenian navy. Later, they laid siege to Athens. Without a fleet to bring supplies, many people in the city starved. In 404 BCE, the Athenians surrendered, bringing the war to an end.

Write a battle report

Imagine that you are Conon, commander of one of the few Athenian ships to survive the Battle of Aegospotami. You have to send a report of the battle to Athens, to prepare people for what is to come. It is bad news, so choose your language carefully, while giving the facts.

An artist's impression of the Battle of Aegospotami.

27

The Trojan War

The story of the Trojan War is told by the great Greek poet, Homer (see below). He describes how the city of Troy was destroyed by the Greeks after a long siege. The war began when Paris, a prince of Troy, eloped with Helen, the wife of Menelaus, King of Sparta. The Greeks sent a huge fleet of ships to bring her back.

A replica of the Trojan Horse.

WAR POETRY

Homer wrote two long poems about the Trojan War. They are called *The Iliad* and *The Odyssey*, and were probably composed in the 700s BCE. *The Iliad* tells of the last few weeks of the war, and focuses on Achilles, the greatest Greek hero. *The Odyssey* describes the danger-filled journey of Odysseus, as he tries to return home after the war.

A wooden horse

For ten years, the war raged on, with heroic deeds on both sides. Paris and many others were killed. Then Odysseus, King of Ithaca, came up with a clever plan. The Greeks pretended to sail away, but left a huge, wooden horse behind. Hidden inside were Greek soldiers, including Menelaus. The Trojans dragged the horse into the city. That night, the Greeks crept out, and opened the city gates to let the Greek army in. Troy was destroyed. The war was over.

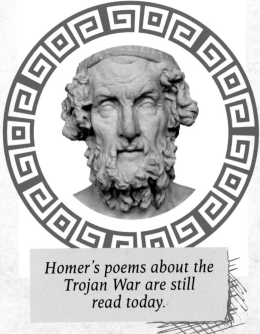

Homer's poems about the Trojan War are still read today.

WRITING HISTORY: Newspaper article

Imagine that you are the war correspondent for a Spartan newspaper. You have been sent to Troy to report on the end of the war, and to interview King Menelaus. Describe what has happened and what you have seen and heard. Remember that you are reporting a glorious victory, so some of your language can be quite over-the-top! The opening text has been written for you.

THE DAILY SPARTAN

SOMETIME IN AROUND 1180 BCE TROY, ASIA MINOR

WAR OVER – HORSE TRICKS TROJANS

AFTER 10 YEARS OF BLOODY FIGHTING, THE TROJAN WAR IS OVER, AND OUR FORCES ARE CELEBRATING A FAMOUS VICTORY.

'THE HORSE TRICK WORKED A TREAT,' KING MENELAUS TOLD ME. 'THEY REALLY DIDN'T SUSPECT A THING.'

WRITING HINTS AND TIPS

- Your article should start with a catchy headline to grab your reader's attention.
- Make the beginning exciting, but leave your readers wanting to know more.
- In the next paragraphs, describe clearly what has happened.
- Finish off your article with a conclusion, drawing all the events together.
- Quotes from eyewitnesses are a brilliant way of bringing the story to life.

Glossary

archaeologist A person who finds and studies places and objects from the past.

aristocrat A member of a rich family that owns land.

citizen A free man who had the right to vote in the government of his city-state.

city-state A Greek city and the land around it.

colony A place away from Greece, where the Greeks settled.

consonant A letter of the alphabet that is not a vowel.

correspondent A person employed to report for a newspaper, television or radio.

culture The customs, beliefs, art and way of life of a particular country or group.

democracy A political system in which all citizens vote to elect polical representatives. In ancient Greek democracy, only well-born men were allowed to vote.

diagnosis What doctors decide is wrong with a patient, after examining them.

elope Run away and get married in secret.

fleet A large group of ships, operating together.

flog To beat with a whip or stick, as punishment.

manoeuvre Move an enemy into a different position by using skill and cunning.

oath A solemn promise.

obituary A notice of the death of a person, often in a newspaper.

offering An object, such as food or drink, that is offered to the gods.

oracle A sacred place where people could consult a god or goddess.

ostracism A special vote to banish unpopular politicians from Athens.

phalanx A block formation in which hoplite soldiers fought.

philosopher A Greek thinker and scholar.

playwright A person who writes plays.

politician A person involved in the government of a place.

recruit A person who has recently joined the army or navy.

sacrifice The offering of a plant, animal, or even human to the gods.

siege Surrounding and attacking a place to cut it off from help and supplies.

temple A place where people can worship the gods.

trireme A Greek warship, with three rows of oars.

Underworld The place where the souls of dead people went.

vowel A letter of the alphabet that is not a consonant. Vowels are a, e, i, o and u.

Further Information

Websites

www.britishmuseum.org/learning/schools_and_teachers/resources/cultures/ancient_greece.aspx
Discover the culture and history of ancient Greece with this British Museum website.

www.ancientgreece.co.uk/
Explore the British Museum's collection of objects from ancient Greece.

www.bbc.co.uk/education/topics/z87tn39
A website filled with maps, facts and images to click on to find out more about ancient Greek life.

Books

Discover Through Craft: Ancient Greece by Anita Ganeri (Franklin Watts, 2016)
Explore!: Ancient Greeks by Jane Bingham (Wayland, 2014)

Every effort has been made by the Publishers to ensure that the websites in this book are suitable for children, that they are of the highest educational value, and that they contain no inappropriate or offensive material. However, because of the nature of the Internet, it is impossible to guarantee that the contents of these sites will not be altered. We strongly advise that Internet access is supervised by a responsible adult.

Index

Writing History

Series contents lists

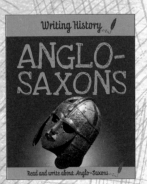

ANGLO-SAXONS

Who were the Anglo-Saxons?
Anglo-Saxon life
Kings and kingdoms
Beliefs and culture
Anglo-Saxons at war
Glossary
Further information
Index

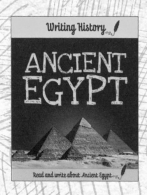

ANCIENT EGYPT

Who were the ancient Egyptians?
Ancient Egyptian life
Pharaohs and wars
Gods and beliefs
Death and the afterlife
Glossary
Further information
Index

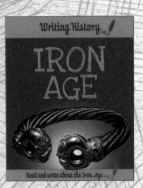

IRON AGE

What was the Iron Age?
Iron Age life
Gods and beliefs
Telling tales
War and warriors
Glossary
Further information
Index

ANCIENT GREECE

Who were the ancient Greeks?
Ancient Greek life
Myths and beliefs
Learning and leisure
Greeks at war
Glossary
Further information
Index

Also in the series:

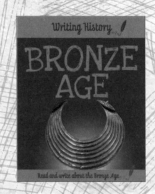

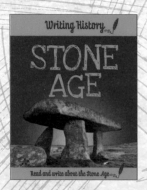